BRITAIN IN OLD PHOTOGRAPHS

CLACTON-ON-SEA

KENNETH WALKER

ALAN SUTTON PUBLISHING LIMITED

Alan Sutton Publishing Limited
Phoenix Mill · Far Thrupp · Stroud
Gloucestershire · GL5 2BU

First published 1995

Copyright © Kenneth Walker, 1995

Cover photograph: front: Pier Avenue early
this century; back: scaffolding being erected on
the beach in the Second World War.

British Library Cataloguing in Publication Data
A catalogue record for this book is available from
the British Library.

ISBN 0-7509-0931-5

Typeset in 9/10 Sabon.
Typesetting and origination by
Alan Sutton Publishing Limited.
Printed in Great Britain by
WBC Limited, Bridgend.

For Margaret

Contents

Nostalgic view – a crowded West Beach in the 1960s.

Introduction

Clacton-on-Sea was born on 18 July 1871; nine days later this happy event was officially celebrated, being favourably reported in *The Times*. But the infant seaside resort consisted of no more than a short pier, reached by a gap in the cliff, at which paddle-steamers plying between London and Ipswich had now begun to call. If its growth was painfully slow by modern standards it was purposefully sure, as will be appreciated from this wide-ranging collection of old photographs recalling its chequered career.

A mile inland from the coast was Great Clacton, sometimes dubbed the town's 'mother village', for here had been the centre of local life for centuries.

The story of Great Clacton, now absorbed in its lusty offspring, is indeed lost in antiquity. Before the Norman Conquest it had been at the centre of a large maritime estate belonging to St Paul's Cathedral. In the Middle Ages it became a perquisite of the successive bishops of London, and they frequently stayed here in their 'stately house', now lost.

Surrounding the village was a network of fields and lanes that stretched down to the sea. At one time the nearby Gunfleet, now Holland Brook, provided a sheltered haven, but it silted up and its estuary was spanned by the sea wall that now forms part of a pleasant footpath between Clacton and Frinton.

During the eighteenth century this rather isolated stretch of coast was the resort of smugglers, and there were occasional clashes with the revenue officers. Then came the Napoleonic Wars and for a time there was a large military encampment on the cliffs at Little Holland. The village experienced unprecedented activity which culminated in 1809–12 with the erection of a number of Martello towers. The four in Clacton still survive.

At this time the area became known as Clacton Beach, and in 1824 an enterprising village innkeeper announced that he had fitted up a machine 'for accommodation of those who are desirous of enjoying the benefits of sea-bathing'. There was, however, no public highway to the shore, but Rosemary Lane (now Rosemary Road) ran close to it, and here were few humble cottages. In 1843 one of them became a beerhouse where passing visitors could obtain refreshment, and where there were occasional dances. A few years later this was converted into a private residence and an adjoining cottage began providing accommodation and became known as The Hotel.

It was to this little hamlet at Clacton Beach that a visitor once travelled down in a carrier's cart, and afterwards recalled that The Hotel 'was but a brick-built labouring gentleman's residence, and the country round looked bare and bleak as far as the eye could reach except a cottage dotted here and there over the landscape, and of less pretensions than the palatial domicile at which we had alighted'. He discovered the sea 'through a sort of gully in what then turned out to be the cliffs', but he afterwards enjoyed a fortnight in these quiet and modest surroundings.

In 1865 about fifty acres of farmland at this spot were offered for sale; they were acquired by an astute civil engineer, Peter Bruff, then engaged in the construction of the railway to nearby Walton. With a view to establishing a new seaside resort he immediately obtained authority to provide a branch railway to Clacton Beach and to build a pier, but the necessary finance was not forthcoming. Five years later, when these powers were about to lapse, Bruff in some desperation approached the directors of the Woolwich Steam Packet Company whose pleasure steamers plied along the coast. The result was a momentous meeting with the chairman on the beach at Clacton when Bruff secured his company's support in the construction of a pier.

Thus it was that Peter Bruff fathered the new resort so happily born in 1871. Said *The Times*, 'That being an entirely new creation, and not the adaption of an existing town, none of the evils inseparable from old watering places will be allowed to exist in it. There will be no slums, nor any object that can offend the eye.' The town indeed began as a decorous Victorian resort, with villas occupied by genteel families, and hotels and boarding establishments visited regularly by good bourgeois folk. But the creation of bank holidays, also in 1871, was to introduce a conflicting element destined to remain, namely the excursionist.

By the time of the First World War Clacton was well established. A town of some ten thousand inhabitants, it had managed to accommodate the fringe of society on the one hand and the brash day-tripper on the other. There was, too, a certain civic pride in its small district council, a remarkable body in that in addition to the normal functions of a local authority it controlled the gas, water and electricity undertakings, and was responsible for protecting the vulnerable coastline with a costly system of sea defence.

Between the wars Clacton continued to expand, and the thousands of summer visitors who came by rail and sea were swelled by an increasing number who travelled by car and motor coach. Then in 1940, during the Second World War, Clacton suddenly became a front-line town. Visitors were banned, and residents were encouraged to leave. It was a bitter blow and life was never quite the same again. For a time, indeed, holiday-makers once more thronged its beaches, but the changing pattern of life meant the closure of many hotels and the provision of more superficial attractions. Meanwhile, however, the town has continued to expand as a residential resort, but with local industry to supplement its seaside amenities. Sadly, with local government reorganization in 1974 the town was too small to retain its independence, and too large to qualify for a town council.

Clacton once displayed under its armorial bearings the motto '*Lux, Salubritas, Felicitas*'. Few may have known its meaning, but 'Light, Health and Happiness' seems to embody the resort's buoyant carefree spirit that it has displayed to the outside world – a town that has everything to offer.

Section One

MOTHER VILLAGE

Great Clacton Street early this century. The Queen's Head with its delightful bow window survives, but the elegant Mansion House and quaint cottages have gone. The former King's Head inn, at the corner of Old Road, is on the left.

The ancient parish church of St John the Baptist, Great Clacton. This photograph must date from about 1860, before the building was restored in the Norman style.

Great Clacton Hall Farm, which adjoined the church. This photograph was taken in 1939 from the site of Ravensdale when the area still retained its rural atmosphere. Here are now a superstore and a car park.

The very old highway that linked Great Clacton on the west side with St Osyth and its once influential abbey. It is now a busy traffic route known as St John's Road, and only the far cottage will be recognized, surrounded by modern development. When the photograph was taken early this century this spot was called the Potash.

Valley Road looking towards the village centre at about the same time. The old forge, with its cottage, is on the right, and Eaglehurst is on the left. A photographer was apparently still regarded with curiosity!

An old wheelwright's workshop on the North Road out of the village, photographed in 1940. It was long occupied by the Granger family: Great Clacton Garage now stands on the site.

The narrow entrance to Old Road by the Ship Inn at the turn of the century. It meandered down to the coast and for a long time served as the main route to Clacton-on-Sea. The windmill is just visible.

THE LONDON COACH LEAVING GREAT CLACTON
SALUTING THE CLACTON BELLE

A picture painted in 1897 to adorn a wall of the former Grand Hotel at Clacton. The Ship Inn is carefully depicted, but some imagination has been used in introducing a London coach. The scene captures some of the activity which the village must have experienced during the Napoleonic Wars, but it was never served by a coach-and-four.

Bringing in the hay. The village is in the distance in this peaceful landscape of about 1900. On the left is Hill House in Old Road, now occupied by Bowens International. The area has been long covered with houses.

A closer view of the post-type windmill on the site of modern Windmill Park. The photograph shows it in a sorry state shortly before its demolition in 1918.

Two ancient cottages a little farther down Old Road which, prior to 1838, had been the village workhouse. The inmates of the workhouse, up to thirty in number, were subject to a rigid discipline. The cottages were apparently occupied separately by men and women. The photograph dates from 1940.

The Queen's Arms at Magdalen Green, late nineteenth century. The small alehouse, between the village and the sea, had been enlarged to cater for travellers to the coast.

One of Clacton's Martello towers, whose grounds became a popular venue for parties, as shown in this print of 1880. Before Clacton-on-Sea was developed this Martello tower, erected within a moat in 1809–12, was the only building by the shore; it now stands on the Marine Parade.

The Martello tower by the present golf course, c. 1912. In the foreground are the guardhouse and magazine, remains of its outer defences which have since been submerged by the sea, together with Eastness, the former promontory on which they stood.

VICTORIAN

INFANCY

Rosemary Lane, now Rosemary Road, in 1877. For some years before Clacton-on-Sea was born in 1871 occasional visitors came to Clacton Beach, as it was then called. There were a few cottages in Rosemary Lane, a short distance from the shore, one of which served for a time as an alehouse. Later, Rosemary Cottage, on the left of this photograph, provided accommodation for visitors. It has now gone, but beyond can be seen the new Osborne Hotel, now the Lord Nelson.

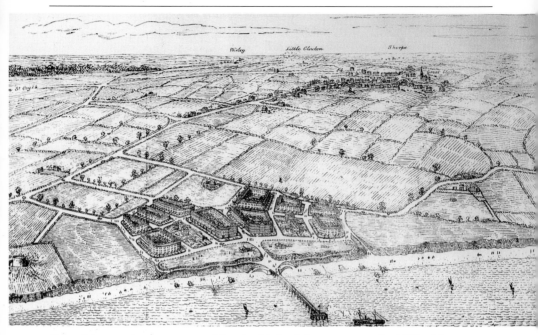

One of the two layouts prepared for the birth of the new resort in 1871: this one was partly adopted. The Martello tower is on the left, and Rosemary Lane borders the projected development. Old Road leads inland to the distant village of Great Clacton.

The Royal Hotel, which opened in 1872, standing in isolation on the cliff top. The Pier, reached by a rough gap in the cliff, was only 12 feet wide, and at first was too short for visiting paddle-steamers to berth at low tide. When the hotel was opened the chairman tactlessly claimed it would 'no doubt prove satisfactory to those visitors who desire to exile themselves from society of every description'! It was gradually enlarged to its present size. Both photographs must date from 1872.

Two villas erected in Pier Avenue behind the Royal Hotel. Behind them are the Public Hall Buildings, opened in 1877, here seen in the course of construction.

The Public Hall Buildings soon after completion in 1877, with open fields opposite. The centre door gave access to the Public Hall. The block was destroyed by fire in 1939.

North Avenue, now Station Road, which formed part of the main approach to the Pier. When this photograph was taken in about 1877 the road was still obstructed by old hedgerow trees. The two houses on the left now form part of a commercial development; the shop on the corner of Pallister Road to the right was then a bakery and the town's first post office.

One of the first houses, Rose Cottage in Rosemary Lane, between the Osborne and Imperial Hotels, c. 1900. It became one of several licensed premises opened in this road – they were banned on the new estate to avoid competition with the Royal Hotel. As a result, it became known as Beer Lane!

James Harman, surveyor and local entrepreneur, who came to live in the little town in 1874. He was actively involved in nearly every aspect of its early development, but later turned his attention to Frinton.

James Harman's hall and office in Orwell Road, adjoining Marine Parade, built soon after his arrival. The hall was variously used as a lecture room, church, telegraph office and bank. When this photograph was taken in about 1900 it was used as a furniture store by his son, Clement Harman, father of a Lord Mayor of London, and the office was occupied by another son, John, an estate agent. Some will recall the Geisha Tea Rooms here.

Looking eastwards across Pier Gap, *c.* 1878. Harman's building is visible on the left, and his house is in the far distance. Little has been done to improve the cliffs, which are slipping into the sea. The hut was built over a sluice which released sewage at high tide!

A few years later: the first sea wall has just been built, and the area tidied up. The flagstaff was an essential feature of a seaside town; it is still in place, though sadly truncated.

An artist's impression of the ceremonial launching of the town's first lifeboat in July 1878. The occasion attracted thousands of spectators, and was long remembered afterwards. There were frequent wrecks on the offshore sands and the coastguards had previously maintained a rescue boat. This new vessel was a gift of the Freemasons to the RNLI and was named *Albert Edward* after their Grand Master, the Prince of Wales.

Six chestnut Suffolk horses drawing the *Albert Edward* down to the water's edge. The ceremony was presided over by Lord Skelmersdale, and it was probably from his carriage that the photographer took this picture.

The first *Albert Edward* lifeboat at sea. Tragically it sank in 1884 with the loss of two boatmen.

The lifeboat as the centrepiece of a ceremony outside the boathouse in Anglefield in the 1890s. The town was proud of its lifeboat.

St Paul's Parish Church standing isolated in the fields some years after it was opened in 1875. It was constructed in concrete with sand from the beach. In the distance is Crossley House on the Marine Parade, originally home of James Harman and later of General William Booth, founder of the Salvation Army.

The stone-laying ceremony at Christ Church in September 1886. For many years it jointly served Congregationalists and Baptists and is now a United Reformed Church. The Wesleyan Methodists were already well established in the town.

Marine Parade East, 1880. This leisurely scene is typical of the Victorian seaside. In the foreground Eagle Gap led up through the cliff into the wide sweep of Beach Road. It was filled in four years later.

A typical Victorian beach scene, *c.* 1887. The photographers have cameras at the ready with dark tents to process their plates, and the boatmen await customers. In the distance are a few cumbersome bathing machines, and the cliffs are crumbling down on to the sand.

The single railway track between Clacton and Thorpe, which was opened in July 1882. Here is the first train which travelled between the two stations; it consisted of a pair of coaches and a guard's van. Only railway staff and children appear to be standing on the platform as the station master hands the driver the tablet giving clearance on the single line.

Cottages built in 1888 for the coastguards in Tower Road when their station was transferred from the lower end of Wash Lane to the adjoining Martello tower. Most of the cottages have now been demolished.

Thoroughgood House, photographed here in 1940 when occupied by its last resident, debonair Percy King. The town first spread eastwards across the fields of Thorogood Farm, and the Georgian farmhouse became a private residence.

Wash Farm or Washford House early in the present century, when the town extended westwards across its fields. The house became a gracious family home, and the scene of a number of social occasions before the Second World War. It was demolished in 1970, and Washford Gardens was developed on its site.

Section Three

EDWARDIAN
ADOLESCENCE

One of the famous Belle boats disembarking passengers at the end of the Pier while another

crowd waits to board her, early this century. By the 1880s the paddle-steamers were

bringing visitors in their thousands, some for the day, some to stay.

OVER 10 HOURS <u>AT THE</u> SEA-SIDE!

J. CUBITT'S Fifth Annual

TO

CLACTON ON SEA

(By a Special Through Train,)

WILL TAKE PLACE ON

WEDNESDAY JULY 10TH, 1889.

STARTING FROM:

LOUGHTON   BUCKHURST HILL

7.25, A.M.   **7.30, A.M.**

WOODFORD   GEORGE LANE,

7.35, A.M.   **7.40, A.M.**

Returning from CLACTON-ON-SEA at 8.10, p.m., arriving home about 10.30, p.m.

☞ RETURN TICKETS :

Loughton and Buckhurst Hill   - - -   **3s. 6d.**
Woodford and George Lane - - - -   **3s. 3d.**

CHILDREN UNDER FOURTEEN HALF PRICE.

All Tickets sold in Loughton will benefit Loughton Sunday Schools. Tickets can be obtained of Mr. Nathan, Loughton; and Miss. Pearce, Post Office, George Lane; or of Mr. Cubitt, George Lane and Buckhurst Hill.

TICKETS SHOULD BE OBTAINED EARLY TO AVOID OVERCROWDING.

A typical poster that speaks for itself: the railway, too, brought swarms of excursionists during the summer season.

The Pier, *c.* 1885. It was still a narrow wooden structure but it was extended beyond its original hammer head, and canted berthing arms were added.

Ten years later and considerable improvements are evident. Hot and cold sea water baths have been provided each side of the Pier entrance – gents on the left, ladies on the right – and the Pavilion theatre with its balcony dominates the Pier head. The two-funneled *Koh-i-Nor*, the most luxurious of the paddlers, appears to be awaiting the departure of its rival, a Belle steamer.

The Pier under snow, with the rowing boats literally in cold storage, *c.* 1912.

A busier scene with a fishing party grouped at the Pier entrance, *c.* 1900. It was probably the occasion of the annual Whiting Feast, then held each November.

Pier Gap, here shown lined with lock-up shops. The photograph must have been taken in 1893 when the Pier Pavilion was nearing completion. The kiosk on the cliff top housed a camera obscura, a form of entertainment where panoramic views were projected on to a screen from a revolving lens in the roof.

Local musician Henry Baynton conducting the Pier Pavilion Orchestra at the turn of the century. The stage décor is reminiscent of a Victorian music hall.

'Professor' George Webb riding his bicycle over the end of the Pier, *c*. 1906. George Webb was one of those memorable local characters whose activities included stunt diving for the entertainment of visitors. He would also dive into the sea in a burning sack.

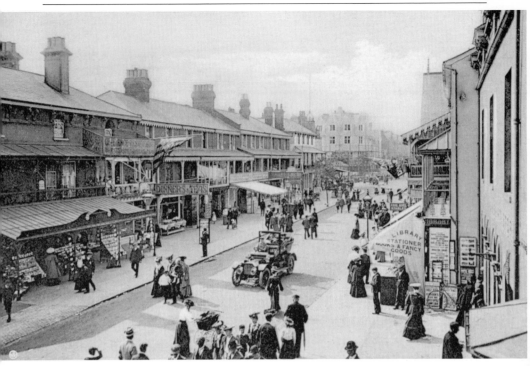

Pier Avenue, which became the town's principal shopping street, 1907. The shops catered for the needs of visitors and are now amusement arcades. Central Buildings and Hotel on the corner of West Avenue were just being completed.

Pier Avenue, from the Royal Hotel to the former Public Hall, with a typical holiday crowd, *c.* 1912.

The Brunswick Family and Commercial Hotel in Pier Avenue at about the same time. It flourished for fifty years, but could not obtain a licence because of the restricted covenant.

An ambitious scheme of 1889 for a clock tower at the junction of Pier Avenue and Station Road, with the Brunswick in the background. A subscriber paying a guinea would have had his name on a step, but the project never got off the ground.

The second *Albert Edward* lifeboat, with crew aboard, being drawn down Pier Avenue by six horses on some festive occasion, *c.* 1900. Grimwades the outfitters on the corner of Station Road will be remembered as Grimwade & Clark, and the building has now been reconstructed as McDonalds. The adjoining villas were converted to shops soon after this photograph was taken.

A view looking up Pier Avenue, with Grimwades on the right, in Edwardian times. Those long-vanished street traders, the boot blacks, are here seen awaiting customers in an age of leather boots and dusty roads. On the left a horse-drawn brake would be taking visitors on a local tour, and beyond is the imposing façade of Electric Parade. This terrace of shops was completed in 1901 and had its own electricity plant before there was any public supply in the town.

The *Swiftsure*, an early motor coach, standing in Pier Avenue, *c.* 1906. It was a Leyland charabanc seating thirty-two passengers, and although 'the waterproof curtains can be fastened during a storm', many considered it to be neither safe nor sure!

A quiet scene by Trinity Church, with only one carriage and a bicycle in view, *c.* 1906. It is now a busy junction. The water tower in the distance was for long a familiar landmark.

Huntsmen gathered outside the Warwick Castle Hotel, *c.* 1900. The hotel, at the top of Pier Avenue, guarded the entrance to the town centre for nearly seventy years.

The church hall built in High Street as St Paul's Church was considered to be too far from the town centre. It replaced an earlier hall which in 1893, on a night prior to a 'monster demonstration against Catholics', was destroyed by fire. It was demolished in 1979.

The large 'tin tabernacle' which temporarily served from 1907 as St James's Church when the west side of the town was being developed. Later it became the church hall and was used for numerous functions until it was demolished in 1984.

Marine Parade West, *c.* 1906. A solitary motor car appears to have been halted by a policeman so that the marching bandsmen may cross towards Pier Gap. Hackney carriages are awaiting hire.

The West Beach just below the Parade at about the same time. Jockey scales are in the foreground; traders' booths, a concert stage and bathing machines are in the distance. Barges were then unloaded on the foreshore among the visitors.

High tide on the West Beach, *c.* 1910: the audience have to stand on the lower promenade to watch the concert. The noise of the sea water pumping plant in the building at the rear cannot have helped.

A standpipe in Vista Road, one of many to which sea water was distributed throughout the town. Thence it was taken in carts to water dusty roads or flush sewers, thus saving treated water. Some local residents were also supplied.

Jetty and steam crane below Wash Lane. Constructed in 1898, and intended for the unloading of barges delivering building and other materials, it proved unsuitable, and barges continued to land on the shore. The Union Jack flies above the Jolly Coons' concert stage.

The Cottage Hospital, built and maintained by voluntary subscription, just after it was opened in 1899. It accommodated seven patients, and still forms part of the town's large hospital complex.

The Palace Theatre adjoining the Martello tower on the Marine Parade. Its opening in 1906 coincided with the inauguration of the town's electricity supply. The site is now absorbed into the hospital.

A veritable Disneyland behind the theatre. Here is one corner, photographed soon after it was opened, which looks like the outcome of an air raid! Visitors are seated on the Grotto Terrace, and behind are the Pigeons Cote and Indian Tea House. Civilization is glimpsed beyond.

Another corner of this Edwardian extravaganza. Against the background of the Martello tower and theatre are, from left to right, 'An Old English Home', the Japanese Pagoda, a bandstand actually in use and a helter skelter. In the foreground is one of two illuminated fountains. And there was lots more! This shaky enterprise did not survive the First World War.

The jetty, 1905. It had been built at an old landing place at Clacton Wash, once a desolate spot where the sea washed over a marshy area.

Looking beyond the Wash to the West Clacton housing estate just being developed, c. 1905. The water tower is on the skyline, and the former coastguard boathouse stands by the end of Marine Parade.

Photographs of the Golf Club taken soon after the clubhouse was opened in 1909. It now forms part of a much larger building. The other views show golfers on the seventeenth green by an ancient mound, and against the sea wall. The Golf Club established the course on the present site in 1896.

The yacht *Isidora*, of Dublin, cast ashore on a nearby beach in February 1906. It had been abandoned by its crew on the Goodwin Sands and had drifted right across the Thames Estuary. The absence of the crew at first caused considerable speculation in the town.

Programme

of the

First Annual Dinner

of a Branch of the Works Department of
H. M. O. W. at the Customs House;

to be held at

Rigg's Retreat & Winter Gardens,
Clacton-on-Sea.

on SATURDAY, JULY 12th, 1913.

Chairman	Mr. H. Lipscombe.
Vice-Chairman ..	Mr. T. Lothian.
Secretary	Mr. W. Davis.

Train leaves Liverpool Street, 7.25 a.m.
Return Train leaves Clacton-on-Sea, 7.40 p.m.
Dinner at 12 o'clock. prompt.

Menu.

JOINTS :

Roast Lamb and Mint Sauce.
Roast Beef and Horseradish.

POULTRY :

Roast Chicken and Ham.

VEGETABLES :

New Potatoes, Green Peas,
Cauliflower or Cabbage.

SWEETS :

Fruit Tarts, Custards, Jellies,
Blanc Mange, etc.

Cheese, Salads.

Ragtime Concert.

Programme.

Opened by W. Davis and J. Eames
" Pathetic Duet."

Song	Character	C. Dennison
Song	Ragtime Cowboy	G. Taylor
Song	Hush don't wake the Baby	W. Collins
Song	Ballad	H. Lipscombe
Recitation	The Soldier's Story	G. Merryman
Comic Song	Ragtime Joe	J. Goode
Band	Selection	A. Webb & Co.
Sketch	Dodging It	G. Ingley. Fulcha, Pickton & Weeks
Character Song	On the Anvil	by Gwyn. Hurran & Co.
Song	Everybody's doing it	C. Duffin

Chairman ... . ANYBODY
Vice-Chairman ... ... HIS PAL.

" Silver Collection."

Usual Toasts.

A typical menu and programme for a Rigg's Retreat and Winter Gardens function, 1913. Rigg's Retreat and Winter Gardens, near St James's Church, catered for large excursion parties, with more than a thousand visitors occasionally attending at one time. There was a resident orchestra in which the world-famous violinist, Lionel Tertis, played in his youth.

A large party having tea in Rigg's Retreat at the turn of the century.

The Retreat Orchestra, led by manager and violinist George Badger. Tertis recalled that he was 'an extraordinary corpulent man . . . he was obliged to loosen and readjust his braces, for only in this way, so he explained, could he reach the G-string with his bow with any degree of comfort'.

Clacton's first fire engine, purchased by the local authority in 1894, which served the town for twenty-seven years. It was drawn by two horses and was provided with a steam pump.

The excitement in August 1906 as the fire brigade leaves the fire station in Old Road to answer a call. Steam pours from the boiler and boys stand by with their bicycles ready to follow the engine to the blaze.

A breezy day, *c.* 1912: the poke-bonnet in the foreground looks secure, but not the girls' hats! The view is looking eastwards across Pier Gap towards the Bandstand on the cliff top.

The summer season in full swing, *c.* 1911. The Belle steamers now had a monopoly, but there had been clashes between two companies and a fracas at the flagstaff when attempts were made to hoist rival flags. As a result the staff was long enclosed by iron railings, as seen in this picture.

A leisurely Edwardian scene looking across towards the Royal Hotel. A lady in the foreground appears to be engrossed in her embroidery.

Colne Road, just beyond the Royal Hotel, early this century. Here the town first developed with a cluster of villas 'chiefly in the homely barge-boarded gable style of the Early Victorian suburb', as noted by Pevsner. Lorne House on the right was replaced by Cordys restaurant in the 1930s. The town clock is in the distance.

Two cannon in Anglefield Garden being ceremoniously unmasked in August 1906 to celebrate (better late than never) the Trafalgar centenary. The guns had been part of the defence of the Parade Martello tower and were dug out of the cliff.

Looking across Anglefield towards the Lifeboat House and Christ Church with its spire (now sadly removed). The guns visible in this photograph were removed during the First World War for fear Clacton should be attacked as a fortified town!

Thomas Lilley JP, chairman of Lilley & Skinner, who at the turn of the century was the doyen of Clacton society. He died in 1916 after a local association of thirty-five years, but some of his large family continued their link with the town. Partner William Skinner was also once a resident.

Lilley's home, Holland House, which was the largest private residence in Clacton and stood within extensive ornamental grounds. The house has long been converted to flats, and the grounds built over. The great gates now stand isolated, a memorial to times past.

The annual Essex Agricultural Show, which was held at West Clacton in June 1900 through the influence of Lilley and others. It was a notable occasion for the small town, and it was honoured by the presence of the Lord Mayor of London. At the railway station he boarded his own carriage which had been brought down the previous day, and here he and his wife are being driven down Station Road under a triumphal arch. The mace-bearer sits in front.

The workmen employed in the building of the former prestigious Grand Hotel, seen here shortly before it was opened in 1897. The work must have been labour-intensive for there appear to be at least 139 men assembled round the main entrance. The hotel boasted electric light throughout, an electric lift and a ladies' orchestra that performed twice daily throughout the year. The proprietors, the Grant family, were closely connected to the owners of Harrods who helped to finance it. Every Boxing Day crowds converged on the hotel to witness a meet of the Essex and Suffolk Hounds. The building is now occupied by the Colchester Institute.

The meet outside the Grand Hotel, *c.* 1908.

The lounge, typical of the Grand's Edwardian décor.

David Cripps Preston of Dulwich who, at the turn of the century, acquired much of the ancient parish of Little Holland immediately east of the town. His scheme for a new seaside resort was slow to develop, but he was the pioneer of Holland-on-Sea, now a part of Clacton. He died in 1925.

Bennett's Farm at the time Preston acquired it. The house, long since demolished, stood by a lane on the site of York Road which led to a gap in the cliffs.

The gap in the cliffs at the end of York Road, probably once used by smugglers and here seen partly eroded in the 1920s.

The sluice house at the outfall of Holland Brook where refreshments could be obtained on the cliff top walk between Clacton and Frinton. In the Middle Ages the brook had a large estuary forming a port behind Little Holland.

Frinton Road early this century. Little Holland Post Office, at the corner of Kings Avenue, is on the right, and St Bartholomew's Church is on the left.

St Bartholomew's Church, Holland-on-Sea's first parish church, which opened in 1903 and served for twenty-five years.

French pioneer airman Salmet seen in front of his monoplane after landing at Great Clacton in August 1912. A large crowd was attracted to the spot to see this rare flying machine.

The reconstructed lower promenade west of the Pier being ceremoniously opened by the Earl of Warwick, Lord Lieutenant of Essex, in July 1912. The name King's Parade, adopted at the time of the coronation the previous year, is no longer used.

Excavation for a sunken amphitheatre on the site of the Bandstand, 1913. The need for an entertainment pavilion had long been felt.

The construction at the same time of a pedestrian bridge across Pier Gap. The unsightly shops on each side of Pier Gap were removed as part of the same project: the whole was designed by Council Surveyor Daniel Bowe.

The scheme being opened in May 1914 by the Sheriff of the City of London, who is seen here proceeding from the bridge to the new Pavilion during the ceremony. The triumphal arch is again in evidence!

Council Chairman Lilley addressing the invited audience at the opening. The bandstand had been re-erected at the lower level. The future for the town seemed rosy, but in two months came the First World War. . . .

The town's first purpose-built cinema, the Kinema in West Avenue. Opened in 1913, it flourished for nearly fifty years. The programme from 31 May 1934 was Lee Tracy in *Turn Back the Clock* and Herbert Marshall in *Solitaire Man*. Happy days!

Section Four

WARTIME SERVICE

Clacton invaded! The Royal Field Artillery bringing guns ashore during the famous

manoeuvres of September 1904, a prelude to the First World War.

A postcard view of the West Cliff, catching a glimpse of the mock invasion in 1904 and the crowd of holidaymakers which it attracted.

A closer view of the departing enemy, keenly watched from the promenade. The manoeuvres were intended to assess Britain's defences when imperial Germany appeared threatening. They were attended by a distinguished gathering of officers and diplomats, both British and foreign, headed by the Duke of Connaught, the King's brother.

The Duke and his entourage mingled with a seething crowd of East End trippers, mountebanks and shell-fish vendors on the beach. The scene must have resembled a Gilbertian farce. Cameras were at the ready, and here a spectator from behind a concert platform has snapped a general emerging from a bathing machine.

Obelisk recording the presence at Little Holland of the Duke of Connaught's family during the manoeuvres. It was erected by David Preston on his desolate cliff top in the hope that it might give a boost to his projected holiday resort at Little Holland. It had long been broken up when it was replaced by the present memorial stone in 1971.

Churchill's unintended visit to Clacton. In April 1914 a seaplane conveying Winston Churchill, First Lord of the Admiralty, from Felixstowe, made a forced landing on the beach. The poor man was assailed by suffragettes and took refuge on the nearby Jetty while waiting for a replacement. He is seen here departing on the nearer plane, with the stranded aircraft just beyond it.

A holiday crowd gathering round a seaplane beached near the Pier. At the end of July 1914 aircraft from Felixstowe and Sheerness were actively patrolling the coast under the shadow of impending war.

A troop of the Essex Imperial Yeomanry riding through the town centre, probably in 1904. Each summer troops were encamped in the area.

The annual camp west of the town early this century. The former water tower is on the skyline and Wash Farm is in the middle distance. On one such postcard a soldier wrote to his young lady: 'If you were here today I would take you out as I have got a holiday.' The poor chap probably never did – it is dated 3 August 1914 and the next day war broke out.

Soldiers placing mines beneath the Pier decking in preparation for the German invasion. The First World War brought a halt to the town's progress, but it enjoyed limited summer seasons in spite of the fear of invasion.

A totally inadequate trench excavated in the grounds of the Middlesex Hospital Convalescent Home in Holland Road to provide shelter from possible bombardment from the sea. The few soldiers in this picture appear to be outnumbered! Thousands of wounded soldiers were brought to the home to recuperate.

A fine view of Great Clacton Street during the war looking towards the former King's Head Inn. Soldiers were continually marching through the town.

A detachment of the Essex Cyclists Battalion stationed at the Jay Wick Martello tower. One of the men depicted sent this postcard in May 1915, observing, 'This is our little grey home in the west.' Note the four cycles.

Church Parade in the new Band Pavilion. From a nearby turret King George V reviewed troops in 1916, the only visit ever paid to the town by a reigning monarch.

The town was *en fête* in July 1919 to celebrate Peace Day. In the morning there was a carnival procession, here attracting large crowds in Pier Avenue.

A children's entertainment in the Band Pavilion in the afternoon. Members of St Osyth Road School are in the foreground, probably standing for the National Anthem.

High Street, *c.* 1915, in sharp contrast to the bustle of the present day. The procession may have been from a local children's home; the collecting boxes are in evidence.

The dignified war memorial surmounted by the figure of Victory looking seawards. This photograph was taken shortly after the memorial was dedicated in 1924 when the life of the town had returned to normal.

Section Five

GEORGIAN
MATURITY

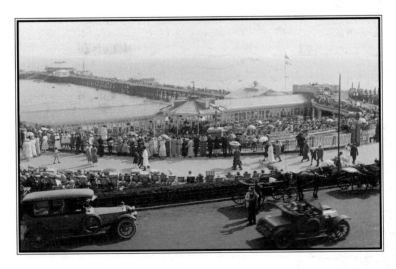

*A nostalgic view, c. 1925. There are still many people whose memories go back to those
inter-war years when, during all too short summer seasons, the many hotels were full of
visitors and coaches brought in thousands of day-trippers. The sound of music wafted
across the promenades from the Band Pavilion as crowds strolled by in the sun – it always
seemed to be shining in those days.*

The centre of the town, *c.* 1920. The large building towards the left is the Kinema in West Avenue. The glass screen on the seaward side of the Bank Pavilion was a veritable suntrap.

The town, 1920. This aerial photograph shows that the extent of the town was considerably less than it is today. Nearly all the buildings along the Marine Parade were being turned into hotels or boarding establishments.

Ernest Kingsman. The prosperity of Clacton between the wars owed much to Ernest Kingsman and his family. In 1922 he took over a pier that was almost derelict, and in the succeeding years was continually improving and extending it so that it became world-famous. He was more often seen in his characteristic beret.

The Pier, showing the improvements well under way, c. 1930. The scene is now hardly recognizable, for the entrance has since been entirely reconstructed, and the Ocean Theatre on the right, the Crystal Casino amusement arcade in the centre and the Childrens' Theatre in the distance have all been demolished.

The original Blue Lagoon dance hall, one of the first additions to the Pier, on the left of the entrance. Once personally decorated each season by the Kingsman family, it was replaced in 1934. It is probably Teddy Dobbs' memorable dance band on the stage.

Ernest Kingsman's wife Ada, seen here (centre front) with a group of glamorous chorus girls in the 1930s. She was a little old-fashioned looking lady, but each year she produced the popular Ocean Revue in the former Ocean Theatre.

The popular childrens' entertainer Clown Bertram in 1939. He had his own theatre at the end of the Pier.

Also at the end of the Pier in 1939, the Ramblas, an alfresco concert party. They were finally disbanded in 1964.

A unique view of the Pier from Steel Stella, the big dipper, 1939.

The former *Southend Belle*, one of a famous fleet, purchased by Kingsman in 1929 and renamed *Laguna Belle*. She plied to and from the Pier for some years.

The *Yarmouth Belle*, which became the *Queen of Southend*, disembarking the first passengers to land at the new Pier berthing arm in 1934. The holiday crowd is typical: it looks from their luggage that some are planning to stay.

The top of Pier Gap just before the Second World War. Motor traffic was steadily increasing, and a policeman was always on duty during the summer months. We can see from this photograph that he stood on a platform for better control.

Marshall's Amusements below the former Brunswick Hotel in Pier Avenue, soon after it was opened in the early 1930s. It was the first of several amusement arcades in the town centre.

Amusement kiosks and a pavilion on the Jetty, which had become absorbed in the West Clacton Estate pleasure complex.

Two boating lakes formed in the old marshy area behind Clacton Wash, for paddle boats to the left and rowing boats to the right.

Another view of the West Clacton Estate, *c.* 1927. Here is a fine display of period cars, with a camping site and putting greens beyond. The town was spreading on the far side of Park Way, just visible on the right.

A lively beach scene looking westwards from the Jetty. This is a photograph taken before Butlins was established here in 1938.

Jay Wick farmhouse, further west beyond the golf course. This ancient farm was acquired in 1928 by Frank Stedman and laid out as a seaside estate known as Jaywick Sands. Here is the old house abandoned in the new development; it has since been demolished.

View of Jaywick Sands, looking from the sea wall up the original farm track of Meadow Way, *c.* 1938. Jaywick began with a few houses near the sea but soon became a township of chalets, many of them permanent homes. There was already a direct service to London from the coach station visible on the left of the picture.

Jaywick, looking from Lion Point back towards Clacton, *c.* 1938.

The Brooklands section of Jaywick, built on former saltings and in front of the old sea wall. This photograph of about 1934 shows the principal road unprotected from the sea which at times flooded over into the roads at the rear. A sea wall was built after the Second World War.

An early view of Beach Road, Jaywick, now Broadway, looking like a Wild West town. The Café Morocco on the right offered dances nightly during the summer season with a London dance band.

The miniature railway, one of the features of Jaywick for a few years before the war. It operated from the station shown here at Crossways to the sea at Tamarisk Way, a distance of about one mile.

Tudor Estate, developed by Stedman behind the old farmhouse at Jaywick. To give it an air of antiquity he placed stocks and a dummy well on a green. This photograph of about 1938 shows the miniature railway in the distance.

A view looking up Burrs Road from Valley Road, 1937. This area still retained its rural atmosphere; the thatched Hillside Cottages on the corner were three hundred years old. They were demolished in 1963 for road improvements.

Further up Burrs Road: the development of a new housing estate. In this photograph of 1935 some of the earliest bungalows had just been completed in characteristic concrete blocks. This was the beginning of Burrsville Park. Ancient Burrs Farmhouse, now the Robert Burre, can be seen in the middle distance.

The extension of the lower promenade towards Holland-on-Sea, *c.* 1938. The usual seaside amenities are on offer but business is hardly brisk! Work is in progress on the distant sea outfall.

Holland-on-Sea, 1920s. Development of this resort was slow: visible here are only a few beach huts perched perilously on the crumbling cliffs.

Harman's Café near Hazelmere Road, where for several years refreshments could be obtained on the walk along the top of the cliffs to Frinton. The open area around Holland-on-Sea was ideal for camping.

Kings Avenue, Holland-on-Sea, the principal route to the sea, just before it was the first road to be made up in 1928. The other roads at Holland-on-Sea were still just rutted tracks. In the foreground is the Café Royal, and beyond lies Dulwich Road and scattered housing.

The Queens Café, Kings Avenue, 1934. Queens Hall is being added at the rear. This little complex stood on the site of Maplin Court until 1972. Note the ice-cream vendor on his tricycle, once a familiar sight.

Hazelton's greengrocer's shop, 1920s. The Hazeltons were pioneer traders at Holland-on-Sea, and here they have extended their business from the main road into the top end of Kings Avenue. Thus began the local shopping centre. Several royal names featured in the little resort, but Kaiser Grove was prudently renamed after the First World War and is now Queensway.

The Princess Helena being replaced by the Roaring Donkey (seen on the right) as the village alehouse of Little Holland, 1934.

The Electric Theatre, the only survivor of an ambitious scheme to provide an amusement centre at Great Clacton. This small cinema, commonly known as a flea-pit, opened in 1922 and survived until the Second World War. The building is now part of Messrs Suswin's premises.

The Odeon Cinema in West Avenue at the time of its opening in 1936. Its terracotta facing was then a characteristic of the Odeon circuit. There were six cinemas operating in the town when this form of entertainment reached its height of popularity just before the war. Note the '3d' just visible on Woolworths shop to the right – the '3d and 6d Stores'! The Odeon was demolished in 1984.

Grays' Glengariff Hotel in Freeland Road. Extensions to the original building are evidence of its popularity: hotels flourished between the wars and many families came regularly each summer to their favourite haunts. Here croquet, miniature golf and quoits are being played on the lawn. The hotel closed in about 1957.

The float representing Glengariff at the 1922 Hospital Carnival. Most of the hotels provided decorated floats for the annual carnival.

Captain Jones and his aeroplane. Many local people obtained their first close view of an aeroplane when Captain Jones began offering pleasure flights from a field on the site of Alton Park School in 1926.

Lloyd George crossing the Venetian Bridge, June 1928. The famous statesman addressed a Liberal rally in the Band Pavilion: the occasion attracted a large crowd, some of whom can be seen in the background.

The little weatherboarded station building, which had served ever since the railway came to Clacton, being superseded by the present station in 1929. The old refreshment room is on the right.

Prince George, later Duke of Kent, naming the new lifeboat *Edward Z. Dresden* after a benefactor, in a ceremony at the end of the Pier, July 1930. Fourth from the right is Sir John Pybus MP, sometime Minister of Transport and the town's most distinguished resident.

A lifeboat service by the beach, mid-1930s. One hopes there were more than five bathers in the congregation!

Prince Arthur of Connaught opening the door of the new Town Hall in April 1931, watched by architect Sir Brumwell Thomas . . .

. . . and the opening ceremony.

Florrie Coleman, MBE, JP, the first lady member of Clacton Council, elected in 1920, and the first lady chairman, pictured here in the 1930s. The wife of a local doctor, Florrie had a gruff and forthright manner that hid a kindly personality. She remained in the town throughout the Second World War – 'I am not leaving Clacton for Hitler or anyone else,' she valiantly declared.

Chairman Sydney Wheeler proclaiming the accession of King Edward VIII in January 1936 from the Town Hall steps. It is said on good authority that, in his embarrassment, he proclaimed Henry VIII as the new monarch, but fortunately someone had cut the amplifier cable. To his right is George T. Lewis, Clerk to the Council for more than forty years.

Amy Wilson laying the foundation stone of the new St Monica's Church of England Public School, watched by the Bishop of Chelmsford, in May 1936. Among several independent schools for girls that once flourished one of the best remembered is St Monica's, where Amy Wilson maintained strict moral discipline. Approaching retirement she negotiated for the school to be taken over by the diocese.

The new St Monica's Church of England Public School in Leas Road. It later took in other premises, but sadly had to close in 1970. Little of this building now remains.

Queen Mary, who was staying in the area, inspecting a parade of ex-service personnel by the war memorial, one bright Sunday afternoon in June 1938. Here she is escorted by Brigadier-General Kincaid-Smith of St Osyth Priory, followed by her brother, the Earl of Athlone, and his Countess, Princess Alice.

The Queen's party leaving for Frinton. There were thousands of visitors in the town and they thronged the Marine Parade to see the Queen.

The most extensive fire in the town's history, one Sunday afternoon in June 1939. It provided a dramatic spectacle for crowds of visitors. Here the flames have gained control of the old Public Hall Buildings in Pier Avenue and are spreading towards the Castle Restaurant at its junction with Station Road.

A hose being played on the smouldering International Stores.

The scene of devastation after the fire. The large store of Lewellens ironmongers had been completely destroyed, but with remarkable dispatch they stocked an empty shop in West Avenue and opened it the next day. This old-established firm continues to trade from these premises.

Against the background of a reconstructed Band Pavilion, Brigadier-General Kincaid-Smith is formally handing over a new St John Ambulance to Superintendent James Cheeld in July 1939. For some weeks Butlins, whose holiday camp had been recently established in the town, had made their own ambulance available for duty along the promenade, and it can be seen here on the right.

Crowds watching girls doing a dumb-bell exercise during a Gala Day at the former Groom's Orphanage in Old Road. The weekly Gala Days, held here for many years each summer, are still remembered by many; one of their highlights was a mock fire.

Section Six

A CASUALTY OF WAR

Evacuee children leaving Clacton, cheered on their way by townspeople, May 1940. Local schools were soon to follow them. On the outbreak of the Second World War in September 1939 the town had received children from more vulnerable areas, but with the threat of enemy invasion the process was reversed. In June 1940 visitors were banned and residents encouraged to leave. A journalist visiting the deserted town wryly commented that boarding houses were now boarded houses.

The Pier was badly damaged by a floating mine in February 1940.

The lifeboat house on the Pier, cut off by the explosion.

The rear of devastated houses in Skelmersdale Road. In May 1940 a crippled enemy plane crashed into a house in Victoria Road (on the left of the picture), and a mine that it was carrying blew up with a deafening explosion, causing extensive damage. Remarkably only two civilians were killed, but many were injured. As the first incident of this nature during the war it received wide if unwelcome publicity.

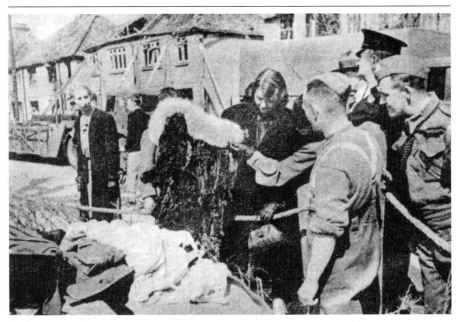

A resident examining her fur coat riddled by flying glass, against the background of shattered homes in Victoria Road.

Whitethorns, Salisbury Road, seriously damaged in June 1940 in the first of many air raids on the town.

Dad's Army marching along an almost deserted Rosemary Road opposite the Carlton: the Home Guard on church parade in August 1940, three months after their formation. This was at the height of the invasion scare.

A pillbox fort slipping down the cliff at Holland-on-Sea at the end of the war.

Tubular steel scaffolding being erected all along the beach to hinder an enemy attempting to land. This unique picture shows the big dipper at Butlins, and the nearby Martello tower from an earlier war. A breach in the Pier, another defensive measure, is just visible on the skyline.

The line of 'dragons' teeth' laid to trap invading tanks. These blocks continued just behind the whole length of Marine Parade. This view, taken from the Martello tower, might be compared with those on pp. 48 and 85, but the Jetty has been demolished as a further safeguard. It was never replaced.

Bomb damage, May 1941. During one of the worst air raids of the war, bombs were dropped near Barclays Bank in the town centre. The damaged bank is seen here towards the left; Ernest Johnson's auctioneer's office on the other side of Rosemary Road was virtually destroyed.

Wagstaff's, the tobacconist, on the opposite corner of Station Road, which was also gutted. Gilders' office is on the right. Fortunately, casualties were limited to seven slightly injured.

The town clock perched perilously above Barclays Bank. This long familiar landmark was removed a few days later, and after the war it was replaced by the present modest clock.

The beach at Holland-on-Sea being used again at the end of the war. The substantial fort, just visible here on the cliff top, remained for a time. During the war thirty-two groynes had to be constructed along this beach to combat coast erosion.

Post-war defenders: a display for children in the moat of the Parade Martello tower in the 1950s.

Section Seven

AGE OF RENEWAL

Butlins Holiday Camp. Butlins had been open only a year when the Second World War

broke out. After the war it came into its own, and its ultimate extent can be appreciated

from this aerial photograph. Its opening had been viewed with misgivings, but its closure in

1983 was a matter of regret.

An early and familiar view of Butlins showing the open-air swimming pool and reception block off West Road.

A less familiar view – the chapel within the holiday camp. It was Billy Butlin's wish that such chapels should be established, and his Clacton Camp was the venue for a number of clergy conferences, the Archbishop of Canterbury attending on one occasion.

The *Sir Godfrey Baring* lifeboat, which replaced the *Edward Z. Dresden* in January 1952. During the previous year this vessel had been displayed at the Festival of Britain, where she is pictured with the Skylon in the background.

The celebrated yachtsman Uffa Fox at the opening of Clacton Sailing Club's new premises at Holland Haven in June 1962. On his left is Commodore Denis Heightman. Since the war sailing has become increasingly popular.

The Great Tide of 1953 when thirty-five of the residents of Jaywick were tragically drowned. The extent of the flooding can be appreciated from this view looking down Golf Green Road towards the sea.

A resident being assisted on to dry land by the police at the junction of Essex Avenue and Brooklands, Jaywick, during the flood.

A police chief inspector and a dog handler patrolling past teenagers in Pier Avenue, Easter 1964. The town received adverse publicity when rival groups of visiting youths clashed and caused mayhem.

A leaflet of 1966 advertising cruises to the *Mi Amigo* (Radio Caroline), *Galaxy* (Radio London) and *Laissez Faire* (Radio England and Radio Britain). For several years pirate radio ships were anchored off the town.

The *Mi Amigo*, which broke her anchor chain during a storm, being driven ashore at Holland-on-Sea, January 1966. In the background are two cranes working on the sea wall.

The original St Paul's Church being demolished following completion of the new building, 1966. As the town approached its centenary a period of renewal commenced.

Claremont, one of the last of the early villas on the Marine Parade, about to give way to new development, mid-1960s.

Acknowledgements

I am indebted to the following:

Alan Ainger • Ken Brown • Clacton and District Local History Society
Clacton Gazette • Brian Essam • Essex County Library • Mary Fairhall
Mervyn Herbert • Imperial War Museum • Roger Kennell
Kenneth Lewellen • David Mantripp • Mary Maskell • Margaret Titford
Peter Underhay • Richard Walker

The title page of the *Clacton Guide*, 1950.

BRITAIN IN OLD PHOTOGRAPHS

To order any of these titles please telephone Littlehampton Book Services on 01903 721596

ALDERNEY

Alderney: A Second Selection, *B Bonnard*

BEDFORDSHIRE

Bedfordshire at Work, *N Lutt*

BERKSHIRE

Maidenhead, *M Hayles & D Hedges*
Around Maidenhead, *M Hayles & B Hedges*
Reading, *P Southerton*
Reading: A Second Selection, *P Southerton*
Sandhurst and Crowthorne, *K Dancy*
Around Slough, *J Hunter & K Hunter*
Around Thatcham, *P Allen*
Around Windsor, *B Hedges*

BUCKINGHAMSHIRE

Buckingham and District, *R Cook*
High Wycombe, *R Goodearl*
Around Stony Stratford, *A Lambert*

CHESHIRE

Cheshire Railways, *M Hitches*
Chester, *S Nichols*

CLWYD

Clwyd Railways, *M Hitches*

CLYDESDALE

Clydesdale, *Lesmahagow Parish Historical Association*

CORNWALL

Cornish Coast, *T Bowden*
Falmouth, *P Gilson*
Lower Fal, *P Gilson*
Around Padstow, *M McCarthy*
Around Penzance, *J Holmes*
Penzance and Newlyn, *J Holmes*
Around Truro, *A Lyne*
Upper Fal, *P Gilson*

CUMBERLAND

Cockermouth and District, *J Bernard Bradbury*
Keswick and the Central Lakes, *J Marsh*
Around Penrith, *F Boyd*
Around Whitehaven, *H Fancy*

DERBYSHIRE

Derby, *D Buxton*
Around Matlock, *D Barton*

DEVON

Colyton and Seaton, *T Gosling*
Dawlish and Teignmouth, *G Gosling*
Devon Aerodromes, *K Saunders*
Exeter, *P Thomas*
Exmouth and Budleigh Salterton, *T Gosling*
From Haldon to Mid-Dartmoor, *T Hall*
Honiton and the Otter Valley, *J Yallop*
Around Kingsbridge, *K Tanner*
Around Seaton and Sidmouth, *T Gosling*
Seaton, Axminster and Lyme Regis, *T Gosling*

DORSET

Around Blandford Forum, *B Cox*
Bournemouth, *M Colman*
Bridport and the Bride Valley, *J Burrell & S Humphries*
Dorchester, *T Gosling*
Around Gillingham, *P Crocker*

DURHAM

Darlington, *G Flynn*
Darlington: A Second Selection, *G Flynn*
Durham People, *M Richardson*
Houghton-le-Spring and Hetton-le-Hole, *K Richardson*
Houghton-le-Spring and Hetton-le-Hole:
 A Second Selection, *K Richardson*
Sunderland, *S Miller & B Bell*
Teesdale, *D Coggins*
Teesdale: A Second Selection, *P Raine*
Weardale, *J Crosby*
Weardale: A Second Selection, *J Crosby*

DYFED

Aberystwyth and North Ceredigion,
 Dyfed Cultural Services Dept
Haverfordwest, *Dyfed Cultural Services Dept*
Upper Tywi Valley, *Dyfed Cultural Services Dept*

ESSEX

Around Grays, *B Evans*

GLOUCESTERSHIRE

Along the Avon from Stratford to Tewkesbury, *J Jeremiah*
Cheltenham: A Second Selection, *R Whiting*
Cheltenham at War, *P Gill*
Cirencester, *J Welsford*
Around Cirencester, *E Cuss & P Griffiths*
Forest, The, *D Mullin*
Gloucester, *J Voyce*
Around Gloucester, *A Sutton*
Gloucester: From the Walwin Collection, *J Voyce*
North Cotswolds, *D Viner*
Severn Vale, *A Sutton*
Stonehouse to Painswick, *A Sutton*
Stroud and the Five Valleys, *S Gardiner & L Padin*
Stroud and the Five Valleys: A Second Selection,
 S Gardiner & L Padin
Stroud's Golden Valley, *S Gardiner & L Padin*
Stroudwater and Thames & Severn Canals,
 E Cuss & S Gardiner
Stroudwater and Thames & Severn Canals: A Second
 Selection, *E Cuss & S Gardiner*
Tewkesbury and the Vale of Gloucester, *C Hilton*
Thornbury to Berkeley, *J Hudson*
Uley, Dursley and Cam, *A Sutton*
Wotton-under-Edge to Chipping Sodbury, *A Sutton*

GWYNEDD

Anglesey, *M Hitches*
Gwynedd Railways, *M Hitches*
Around Llandudno, *M Hitches*
Vale of Conwy, *M Hitches*

HAMPSHIRE

Gosport, *J Sadden*
Portsmouth, *P Rogers & D Francis*

HEREFORDSHIRE

Herefordshire, *A Sandford*

HERTFORDSHIRE

Barnet, *I Norrie*
Hitchin, *A Fleck*
St Albans, *S Mullins*
Stevenage, *M Appleton*

ISLE OF MAN

The Tourist Trophy, *B Snelling*

ISLE OF WIGHT

Newport, *D Parr*
Around Ryde, *D Parr*

JERSEY

Jersey: A Third Selection, *R Lemprière*

KENT

Bexley, *M Scott*
Broadstairs and St Peter's, *J Whyman*
Bromley, Keston and Hayes, *M Scott*
Canterbury: A Second Selection, *D Butler*
Chatham and Gillingham, *P MacDougall*
Chatham Dockyard, *P MacDougall*
Deal, *J Broady*
Early Broadstairs and St Peter's, *B Wootton*
East Kent at War, *D Collyer*
Eltham, *J Kennett*
Folkestone: A Second Selection, *A Taylor & E Rooney*
Goudhurst to Tenterden, *A Guilmant*
Gravesend, *R Hiscock*
Around Gravesham, *R Hiscock & D Grierson*
Herne Bay, *J Hawkins*
Lympne Airport, *D Collyer*
Maidstone, *I Hales*
Margate, *R Clements*
RAF Hawkinge, *R Humphreys*
RAF Manston, *RAF Manston History Club*
RAF Manston: A Second Selection,
 RAF Manston History Club
Ramsgate and Thanet Life, *D Perkins*
Romney Marsh, *E Carpenter*
Sandwich, *C Wanostrocht*
Around Tonbridge, *C Bell*
Tunbridge Wells, *M Rowlands & I Beavis*
Tunbridge Wells: A Second Selection,
 M Rowlands & I Beavis
Around Whitstable, *C Court*
Wingham, Adisham and Littlebourne, *M Crane*

LANCASHIRE

Around Barrow-in-Furness, *J Garbutt & J Marsh*
Blackpool, *C Rothwell*
Bury, *J Hudson*
Chorley and District, *J Smith*
Fleetwood, *C Rothwell*
Heywood, *J Hudson*
Around Kirkham, *C Rothwell*
Lancashire North of the Sands, *J Garbutt & J Marsh*
Around Lancaster, *S Ashworth*
Lytham St Anne's, *C Rothwell*
North Fylde, *C Rothwell*
Radcliffe, *J Hudson*
Rossendale, *B Moore & N Dunnachie*

LEICESTERSHIRE

Around Ashby-de-la-Zouch, *K Hillier*
Charnwood Forest, *I Keil, W Humphrey & D Wix*
Leicester, *D Burton*
Leicester: A Second Selection, *D Burton*
Melton Mowbray, *T Hickman*
Around Melton Mowbray, *T Hickman*
River Soar, *D Wix, P Shacklock & I Keil*
Rutland, *T Clough*
Vale of Belvoir, *T Hickman*
Around the Welland Valley, *S Mastoris*

LINCOLNSHIRE

Grimsby, *J Tierney*
Around Grimsby, *J Tierney*
Grimsby Docks, *J Tierney*
Lincoln, *D Cuppleditch*